The Happy Shepherd

By Jean-Jacques Myard

The essential quick guide to training, handling and living with a German Shepherd Dog.

Copyright © 2022 Jean-Jacques Myard

All rights reserved.

Book Design and Cover Design by:
Jeanna and Bernell Clifford

ISBN:
ISBN- 978-0-578-29138-3

CONTENTS

Introduction	1
Chapter 1 – Why choose a GSD (German Shepherd Dog)	3
Chapter 2 – Many uses of the GSD	6
Chapter 3 – Choosing a puppy	9
Chapter 4 – The early years	12
Chapter 5 – Communication	16
Chapter 6 – Training	18
Chapter 7 – Playing and exercise	26
Chapter 8 – The world and others	27
Chapter 9 – Health and care	30
Chapter 10 – Multiple dogs	32
Chapter 11 – Retirement	34

INTRODUCTION

The first German Shepherd arrived in our family when I was 14 years old. His name was Sheriff. He was a little fur ball with floppy ears, puppy breath, and razor-sharp teeth. I discovered this fabulous breed over the years that followed. We had had dogs before, but none quite like this one. As I was pondering why this breed stood apart so much, I was reminded of the words of my grandfather, who had told me that during World War II, German Shepherds were referred to as "tools."

Over the course of the last four decades, I have had the pleasure to own, train, and work with many German Shepherds, in several countries and in different languages. I started training my first GSD at an obedience and protection school when I was a teenager. Over the years, I have trained all of my own dogs, trained them for others, and all-the-while, educating humans on how to best handle them. Today I have two of them, a brother and a sister, and they just turned 10. They are by far the best companions I have ever had.

What I love about the German Shepherd dog: It is first and foremost a working dog; but also, a loyal companion and member of the family unit. I say first and foremost a working dog because it is just that, the German Shepherd is always working. What the shepherd is not, is a pet, as I will explain in the pages that follow.

The German Shepherd is smart as a whip and it will outsmart you on any given day. I have used these wonderful creatures for protection of people and property, working companions, playing hide and seek, and more recently I have trained them for bear Patrol. Just about everything I know about the German Shepherd dog, the dogs have taught me over the years that I have spent with them. Training school taught me how to properly communicate with GSDs, as well as train them, and over the decades, **the dogs have taught me how they think.**

The intent of this book is to share all I know about this breed in order to facilitate the best relationship between the dog and the owner who chooses a German Shepherd. Some of the information contained herein will apply in part to other shepherd breeds, such as Belgium Shepherds and Shilohs.

This is not so much a training book specifically, but rather an overview of **what to expect if you are choosing a German Shepherd dog**. There are countless in-depth books dedicated to the training aspect, as well as other books for specific training; be it for obedience, herding, search and rescue, police or military.

There are also plenty of other books dedicated to other breeds that you may want to consult if you are wondering what type of dog breed to get.

Throughout the following pages I will often refer to the German shepherd dog as GSD.

CHAPTER 1: WHY CHOOSE A GSD

Many people choose GSDs over other breeds for various reasons. A few of the top choices are a need for a working dog, a protector/guardian, or a companion and family member.

It is important to note that **the GSD is not considered a pet,** as most people understand it. The GSD is a very engaging, intelligent, and energetic dog. It has an excellent temperament, instinct, and strong working desires.

It will require a little bit more attention than other breeds, as it constantly seeks to fulfill some sort of task. However, there are other breeds, such as the Border Collie for example, that require a little bit more attention.

The GSD's goal in life is to please his owner/handler. You can say that they are a one-track-mind dog. They will be happy to always do something for you, even if it is just laying down after you gave them the command. They are undoubtedly one of the easiest breeds to train. Handled properly, a GSD can be the closest, most loving, and trustworthy companion anyone could desire.

Remember that like with all breeds, which have their specific traits, within the GSD breed, all dogs will come with their own, very unique personalities. We cannot assume that since we have a GSD that it's going to be like every other Shepherd. Some might learn fast, others may take longer, some may be more aggressive, while others may be more submissive.

Your GSD will need room to roam, time to play, and a lofty place of their own. The GSD is an excellent addition to any family unit, and will gladly take its place in the hierarchy of all of your household members.

Your GSD will always have their eyes on you, they will be aware of the surrounding environment, sense danger through their senses or instinctually, even while they are sleeping.

GSDs are excellent with kids, other pets, and livestock especially if you get them as a puppy. That way they will have time to grow into the family unit, and figure out their place within it.

The GSD is also an incredibly tolerant and forgiving dog. I once saw a GSD riding on a scooter with his military handler in Thailand. Full speed ahead, tongue flapping in the wind, happy as a kite. GSD's are very proud, elegant, and beautiful creatures.

So if you are considering getting a German shepherd dog make sure you have the proper facilities to care for them. Make sure you also have the time to tend to their needs, as well as the budget for food and vet bills. Don't let it fool you: Expenses can add up quickly between food, vet bills and the occasional kennel, which will be noticeable over a period of years.

WARNING:

Do not get a GSD (or any working dog for that matter) if you do not or cannot train them properly! Without training, you will end up with disaster soup.

If you are considering this breed specifically, there is going to be a commitment you have to make to yourself and to your GSD (if you want a peaceful life and world around you).

Shepherds are extreme shedders. A GSD will shed more hair than any other breed. So be forewarned, you will have to brush your dog often, and you'll still end up with hair everywhere.

Do get a Shepherd if: you have a strong leadership mentality; are willing to educate yourself about the breed and training; have proper facilities; and have the time it takes to train and care for your dog. All for which you'll be rewarded beyond your greatest expectations.

Remember, the GSD is a dog primarily guided by their instinct (as most animals are). Your job is going to be to override those instincts at times in order to keep them under control.

Plan on having a proper training protocol and enforcing it in order to have the best experience for all parties involved. If you can't do that, you most likely will end up with problems.

It is worthy to also note, that of all the German Shepherds I have owned, there are known hip, joint, and gastrointestinal issues that can arise with this breed. No matter how good the breeder is or how expensive the dog, genetic issues can occur, especially for dogs that are overbred. Just so you know.

The **GSD makes for a perfect working dog**: Deep down in their genetic tree is the desire to work and to please. They can be trained for many different uses and fulfill multiple jobs.

These are all the factors to take in when considering owning a GSD. Remember, you are entering into a 10 to 15 year relationship that is going to require some of your time, energy and money.

Taking these factors into consideration will ensure a happy dog and a happy owner. Failure to do so will make your (and your dog's) life miserable.

Overall, considering the trade-off of what you are getting, it is absolutely priceless.

Some of the information you will find here will apply to other breeds of dogs, such as health and care and training/communication. This little book is specifically focused on German Shepherd dogs. Please do add your own dose of common sense for general dog ownership, as you would with any other type of dog.

CHAPTER 2: MANY USES OF THE GSD

Throughout history, there have been many uses for German Shepherd Dogs. In World War II they were "tools". They have been trained to lead the blind, help diabetics or detect explosive devices. They have excellent sensory capabilities that have made them famous throughout history for all kinds of work missions.

Their most common use is for personal protection and guarding of property. But they can also be herders, and **can be trained to fulfill multiple functions**.

I do not need to list all of the search and rescue, police and military uses of these fine dogs.

It should be noted that most dogs will have a specific gene

orientation for specific types of work, in addition to the inherent protection/guard work. With very little effort, we can match dogs to types of work they are more likely to excel in.

For example, my current dog Rio, seems to be interested in cattle and sheep. I therefore deduct that he would have made a fine herding dog. His sister Frida, on the other hand, she's very interested in sniffing things out; she loves to play looking for her ball in the snow. That might make her a good search and rescue/avalanche dog, or any other use requiring a good nose. Regardless, **you can train a GSD for almost any use they are genetically designed for or have a proclivity towards.**

When we can decipher a dog's specific inclination, it is going to make the training that much easier, and will make the dog that much happier. Therefore you will both be happiest.

That said, any German Shepherd dog could fulfill any of those jobs and be happy just "working."

My current GSDs work perimeter control, keeping strangers, bears, and other wildlife off of the immediate property. They have been trained not to chase deer, but to keep bears at bay within the control perimeter. Wildlife needs room to exist too.

Personal and property protection being an inherent genetic trait of all of the GSDs, they rarely have to be trained for that job, but more often than not, **they have to be controlled and instructed** in that endeavor.

I am not a big fan of GSD's being used for crowd control for example, dodging bullets in war, or any other violent form of human activity. Search and rescue dogs who work in the aftermath of earthquakes for example do not necessarily enjoy finding dead bodies. I would not either. So even though they are a good breed for that type of work, one should keep in mind the emotional and physical side-effects of any work on a dog. Dogs have feelings too, Shepherds are no exception.

So when looking for a working dog, please consult literature about which breed is best for which job. Try to match additional traits of the individual dog to his future career; fully knowing that all hard work will have hard consequences on the mind or body of your dog.

The best part about the versatile uses of **the GSD is that they will adapt to any workload and combination.**

Most people have them as companions and/or guardians. They are excellent family members as well. They love to play, love kids, are basically happy to do any job, or just hang out keeping an eye on you and the family.

CHAPTER 3: CHOOSING A PUPPY

Now that you have chosen the GSD breed as your top pick for your needs, you must find a good breeder. That is the most important step number one. Stay away from puppy mills. Good breeders have reviews. Do your own research and **please, take your time**.

If possible, visit the facility, or ask for pictures and/or short videos. **A good breeder will know the attributes of each puppy** and should be able to help you pick one that suits your needs. Meet the puppy's parents if possible, you will be able to tell if they are more active/aggressive or zen/mellow, therefore helping you in your selection. Some people want a mellow family member/protector, others need an energetic workhorse for a specific job.

A quick note here on pure breeds:

Sometimes dogs can be overbred. This can lead to potential diseases and/or issues down the line. Just remember, dogs that are mostly Shepherd, will most likely carry the attributes of the GSD that you are searching for. So please, do not discount saving a dog from the pound that is healthy, mainly Shepherd, and looking for a good home.

If buying a dog from a breeder, ask to verify a clear hip and joint genetic history, in addition to a vet certificate.

If the breeder is not located too far, try to visit the puppy once or twice before acquiring your future companion.

Male or female?

I have had and worked with both. The "she-pherd" female is generally going to be a little more receptive, sensitive and delicate. She's going to learn faster, will work as hard and require a bit less work than a male overall. Some people chose a female to breed. Make sure the genetics are all good, and please follow a proper breeding care/protocol if that's your plan.

Your male GSD, in contrast/complement to the female, will usually show a little more confidence and straightforwardness. He is more likely to be challenging to you at first, especially in the early training process, constantly checking your mental strength. **By the age of 4 months, you are either the boss of him, or he is the boss of you.** This is reversible, of course at that young age, but critical time is wasted if there have been mixed messages sent to the dog.

If you keep him intact, which will for sure influence his drive to work, you can decide if you want to breed him down the line.

If you decide to get a puppy:

Prepare a place in your house for your puppy and plan a budget for food, vet, and kennel. Remember, this is a 10 to 15 year commitment for which you are going to be responsible. Puppies can get big fast, therefore, do not get what will be a large dog if you live in a small apartment. Unless perhaps you are able to take it everywhere with you (working dog, dog for handicapped persons, ect.). Regardless, the dog will need room to roam every day, or he might express his unhappiness in unwelcomed ways, that you will eventually find out.

Advantages of starting with a puppy:

As a puppy, the dog will have an easier time growing up with the other members of the household; whether people or pets. Puppies will be great for kids to play with, however that said, not all dogs/Shepherds like kids throughout their lives. They might love them when they are in the puppy stage and want nothing to do with kids as grown dogs. Many kids have been bitten just for wanting to hug a big fluff ball. So watch how your GSD acts around the presence of other kids, other dogs, and adults alike as he gets older.

Now for the fun part, you get to pick a name! **Choose a name that is preferably short**, such as one or two syllables, which will ease your communication and training.

CHAPTER 4: THE EARLY YEARS

Within the first 2 months of getting your puppy, and subsequent year or two, will pretty much set the roadmap for you and your dog's relationship. This is where all of the most important work is done. The work you will be doing at that time will be quintessential for the rest of your GSD's life.

Your dog will go through **4 pretty distinct phases: Puppy; young dog; young adult; adult.**

Let's start with the puppy stage:

At this age, most of the work you will be doing will be playing. Your dog will learn to communicate with you as he plays, and will learn his first words and commands. It is of the utmost importance that you start establishing this communication channel that will carry on for the rest of your dog's life. We will talk about communication in the following pages.

Of equal importance, is the socializing of your puppy/young dog to all aspects of your life and to the other members of your family, as well as strangers. Your young GSD should have interactions and pettings from other humans. Failure to do so while your dog is young, might result in difficulties which may be impossible to fix later.

Ideally, your growing dog/puppy will have a designated place in the house, in the form of a boarded pen or dog kennel box, with a door. It will have a bed and a water bowl. **It is important for your young dog to have a place that feels safe** and unencumbered from other going-ons inside the house. He will feel safe, comfortable and happy to engage with the rest of the family when he is done resting and invited for supervised play.

Over time, your young dog will just have a bed out of the way of human traffic, positioned where he can see you and the front door if possible.

When getting a new dog, you should **start a routine right away**. Fully knowing that puppies can't hold themselves very long, it will be your responsibility to take him outside as often as possible. If he has a mishap inside his pen or in the house, do not reprimand him; rather take him outside right away. If you take him out before you go to bed, and first thing in the morning, he (and his organs) will get used to that routine.

Make sure you congratulate him when he goes outside by telling him "good boy" or some type of praise.

He does not need a reward (treat) at that point.

Feeding times should also come like clockwork. **The Shepherd likes a schedule, repetition, and consistency.** Choose two times in a day when you will feed him (3 times a day for a puppy until 3 months of age). I like to feed mine at 9 a.m. and 5 p.m. The bowl with food will be with him until he finishes it, and be taken away when he is done. If he does not finish his food, give him a little extra time, then take the bowl away until he figures out that if he doesn't finish his bowl, he might miss out on the other half. If he still doesn't finish his bowl, you're either giving him too much food, or he's got something going on to ask your vet about.

But trust me, puppies and young dogs are very hungry as they are growing and have no problems eating!

As soon as he is done eating, you may take him out for a walk. Your dog will get used to the program of eating and going outside to the bathroom.

This is the time when you **start introducing simple commands** such as sit, come, good dog, etc.

If you are feeding more than one dog, keep them and their bowls separated. Each dog should eat his/her food, in their respective bowls, in the same dedicated feeding area.

The training part, which will be touched upon in the following pages, will be more comprehensive and start with play time. Use the name you have chosen for your dog often when talking to him. Eventually, he will associate the name with himself and respond to it.

Playing will be an essential part of your dog's routine during the day. You want to play with your dog in between meals, but not too much right after meals, which can cause an upset stomach. Playing is important for the dog's physical development as well as for building a relationship between the dog and the owner.

It is important that you start integrating your dog's presence in your household as soon as he gets there, with all the other inhabitants. The kids should play with him, the cat might take its time to warm up to the idea, but over time, all will fall into place.

At this stage in a dog's life, your puppy/young GSD should be either supervised or penned up or in his special place (kennel or crate).

Make sure there is nothing to eat or chew on as puppies are known to get into trouble. **Do not ever share human food with your puppy,** as this will create bad habits.

Make sure you give your dog plenty of affection, through petting, as he loves "the hand," scratching and everything else you would do with any other dog.

Petting your GSD will also allow you to detect any unusual bumps, wounds, ticks or burrs.

Remember, that all **the work you do now will create shortcuts for future training,** as well as make the training a lot easier. All of my dogs executed their basic commands in the first couple months of integration.

As your dog grows out of puppyhood and starts enjoying a little more freedom in the house, watch where he naturally gravitates toward laying down. This will give you clues of where he prefers being. Now if it is right behind the front door, that's not going to work during the daytime, but he might like to sleep there at night, for reasons of his own. Use these clues, in addition to your preferred spot for him; and again, if he can be in a place where he can be out of the way, have his eyes on you and the front door, that would be ideal for everyone.

It is in these early years that **you will discover your dog's personality.** Some are more dominant, others more submissive, and some work-driven. Knowing this will give you a head start for future training and a roadmap for your dog's interaction with the world.

Specific work related training usually starts later, when the dog is 6-8 months old. You will have a head start with the basic obedience training, especially after you have established communication channels.

CHAPTER 5: COMMUNICATION

The most important part of training is going to depend on the degree of communication that you develop with your GSD. **Communication is key**.

The communication channels need to be opened and developed in both directions: You need to be able to communicate to your dog what you want him to do, and you also need to be able to read what your dog is trying to tell you.

This process is self-reinforcing, as your GSD will not only want to execute commands, he will also know that you are attentive to his messages. This will foster a sense of trust between the both of you.

Over time, most communication is done through **eye contact**. So make sure your eyes and his meet often, especially when you are giving him commands.

The training part can be done through verbal commands first, followed by sounds, then followed by gestures. That way you can have three different ways of expressing a command.

Your GSD will also communicate with you in many clever ways that you will have to decipher.

It is important to note that **your GSD is a lot smarter than you will ever think that he is**. He uses all of his senses, including the 6th one, making him aware of more of what is going on than an average human.

I personally have used three different languages, along with signs and little sounds to communicate with all of my dogs. You can even make up words that are specific just for them.

For privacy and security's sake, **only you and other members of your household may give your dogs any commands**. Commands should be kept within the family's private circle. Your "not-a-pet" GSD is a tool with work to do. Strangers should not be able to communicate with your security system.

Once you have established communication with your dog, all commands will be used in a purposeful manner and not for playing circus dog tricks. **As the years go by, you will rarely need commands**. Your dog will instinctively know what you expect of him and will just do what he's supposed to do.

Additionally, your dog will sense your desires and general mood by smelling your knee or your wrist, where your glands are, and figure out everything he needs to know just from that. Same goes for everyone he comes across.

So, if your dog's needs and your needs are communicated, fair and consistently, you will have much greater success in the training process and enjoy a happier life together.

CHAPTER 6: TRAINING

To keep this quick guide short, for now, I'll just share a few words on the subject in order to give you some basic obedience training principles, proper Shepherd conduct, a few shortcuts and basically the "law" as it was taught to me early on.

Training is the part you want to prioritize along with communication, as it will make your life a lot easier and your dog a lot happier. **Communication + Training = Success**.

In addition to the basic information I will share below, I cannot recommend enough that any person considering owning a GSD should get a training manual and/or attend classes if necessary. Ideally you would educate yourself and seek assistance if needed to train your dog. It's really easy to train a GSD, but you have to do it right, or face future setbacks. I am really grateful that I was able to learn at a training school, as well as practice, work, train and read. You will never regret the time spent on that either.

Another couple of options: If you are not capable or confident that you can successfully train your Shepherd, you should either buy one fully trained or hire a trainer that will train your young dog for you in a couple of months.

Start the training as young as possible. It is going to take some time at first, but it will make the difference between a very easy life for you and your dog, or a never-ending uphill battle.

Stay firm, yet gentle. You want to be the boss, but not a slave driver. You want to earn your dog's respect, mainly by having him want to follow your lead.

German Shepherds can learn a command on the first go-around. They are so smart and eager to please; it blows me away how attentive they are. You can train them through play, and they won't even know they are being trained. Playing for them is their early form of learning and communicating. It is how you exchange information, where they can connect with their name, and the basic commands of "sit," "stay," "come," and "no."

Looking over my notes from long ago, I noticed that my second Shepherd got his basic training done by the age of 3 months and 3 weeks: We had a breakthrough moment and he was 100 percent dedicated to me and the training. Whatever hadn't worked perfectly before then, just "clicked."

So be patient, and be forgiving. Don't expect too much out of your puppy, it is the repetitive training for the first couple of months that is going to bring you results. Your GSD is trying as hard as he can to please you, just as you are trying to understand his needs.

Rule number one: **Never repeat a command**. Your word has to be the law, and you do not want to repeat yourself. That way your dog will know there are no other options, that you mean what you say and you are the boss. If your puppy does not reply to "sit" for example, gently help him with the command using your free hand.

Rule number two: **Never, ever hit your dog**. There are many other ways to reprimand, and hitting does more harm than good. Your GSD is so eager to please you that if he makes a mistake or doesn't perform a command, he already knows you're not happy with him. Additionally, he's either testing you because he's a young dog, or trying to tell you something. Never ever raise your hand in a threatening manner, or use any objects to hit, or take your frustration out on your dog. This is basic common sense, but needs to be mentioned because, in one slip-up, you can damage a dog beyond repair.

Reprimand: Assuming you will start with a puppy, and start the training right away, grabbing your dog by the top of the neck and saying "no" - or whichever coded word you chose - should suffice. For reprimanding further if necessary, you can lay your dog down (**firm, yet gentle**), grab and pull on top of his neck and say "no."

If the need for correction involves an object that was chewed on, for example, make sure that the object is right in front of him so he can make the connection.

Catching him in the act of whatever he's doing wrong will have the most impact for a behavior correction.

Over time, your dog will know what is and is not acceptable to you, and there will be very little physical reprimand needed, as words will do just fine. In the end, all will be said with eye contact anyways. And yes, your dog knows the difference between your smiley face and a frown.

You have to **enforce your rules firmly from the start**: Your puppy would never think of talking back to you, but your young dog will if you haven't laid down the law already.

Important note: You need to be the boss by being firm, but make sure you do not over-power your dog to the point that you will break his spirit. You can get your message across with little effort and no violence. Failure to navigate that fine line properly may bring you unpleasant surprises later. **You don't ever want to lose his respect.**

Learn to read your GSD: For example, my dogs never got in the trash or chewed anything up. I got them all the exercise they needed, so they were not hyper. I got them all the bones to chew on, and plenty of love and attention.

Occasionally Rio, my male, would move my shoes around. He wasn't chewing them up, but just telling me he wanted to play, get my attention, or go outside. After I picked up the shoe, I would just look at him, and he wasn't looking too proud. Usually his head low, ears down, and the sorriest look on his face. He knew how I felt about that, and I could tell he was just communicating with me.

Now, it is very important to note, that I did not play with him right away, as he would see it as a reward for **playing musical shoes in my living room**. So I let a little time go by, disconnect from the shoe episode, then take him out or play.

Ideally, you or the same member of your family should be the dedicated trainer. Then you can pass the commands down to other members of the family, making sure they follow the same exact rules. Not taking this into consideration, may ruin your training work, or set you back in the process.

The most important command: Recall (come/heel). If you do not have that one down, you are inviting trouble. Easily teachable with a long leash with a puppy or young dog. Add a treat if a reward is necessary.

Your GSD should always have his own spot wherever you go, in the car, at home, the office or when traveling. That will be his point of reference wherever he is, and a safe refuge from all the goings-on of the world around him. He will know that he cannot get into any trouble there (as he's learning the ropes).

GSDs really like structured order, repetition and performance. Think of it as fine German engineering.

The **basic commands** that all GSDs (and all dogs really) should learn to perform: **Come, heel, sit, stay, no, and go to your spot.**

Verbal rewards, pettings, as well as treats, and playtime should be used often to reinforce your dog's proper behavior.

I have never used a shock collar, nor believe it is necessary for the GSD. To tell you the truth, I am not a big fan of those collars, but I understand that they might have a use for specific needs and certain breeds.

I have used treats for rewards, but not always. Ideally, you should be able to use pettings and verbal rewards, as treats should not always be part of your training. You want your dog to **execute commands even if he doesn't smell a treat in your pocket.**

Quick note on rescued dogs: A rescued GSD will be very happy to be included in a new home. Especially if he comes from a broken home where there was lack of care or abuse. He will recognize the opportunity and be eager to do his best to fit in your pack.

That said, you are going to have to spend a little (or a lot) of extra time figuring him out to understand his strengths, weaknesses or phobias. You will need to keep an extra eye on him for a while to make sure he doesn't get into trouble; like you would with a puppy.

In addition, training an older dog takes a bit more time. Start the routine and start the training ASAP.

Make sure you, yourself, stay the top dog. Don't ever let a new dog challenge you without reprimanding him.

Please keep in mind that not all rescue dogs are suitable for all households or owners.

Command variations: Pick the word of your choosing for each command. In certain applications, you may choose words that only your dog and your family unit recognize. That will keep strangers from being able to give your dog commands.

For example, my dogs know commands in German, French, English, in addition to sounds and gestures. Choose words that are short, preferably one syllable.

Command variations part deux: In addition to eye contact and verbal commands, I like to add other sounds and gestures. It can be very handy if you need to communicate a command quietly. First train with verbal commands, and once your GSD has that verbal command down, start overlapping it with a gesture, at the same time. Once your dog gets both commands as the same, you will be able to use either. For example, I can verbally tell my dog to get to his spot, or point at his spot, or snap my fingers. Either of those will get him to his place.

The best and easiest way to get all the basic training done, is to dedicate 15-20 minutes twice a day to it, preferably after playing so the dog is calmer. **The younger you start the training, the faster it goes, and therefore the sharper the dog will become.**

As a young dog, you can use his name right before the command: that way you get his attention and he knows you're talking to him. Over time, you can just use the desired command without using his name. (Unless you have multiple dogs.)

If your dog is distracted during a training exercise, detour/reroute away from the distraction, then start again. Ideally the area you are starting the training in is free of squirrels, pigeons, or other dogs. When you get deeper into the training, you can, and should, start adding distractions.

Using a leash: Excellent to start, try to have that leash as loose as possible, only tightening when needed. Your dog should never pull on the leash; **you are walking him, he is not walking you!**

Heeling should be done on your left side. I like to hold the leash with my right hand, and use my left hand for petting, executing commands or giving rewards. The leash is in my right hand, goes behind my back, to the dog's collar on my left. Most everyone holds the leash in their left hand. Use what works best for you.

As a puppy, your dog should be allowed to roam the house and property (supervised) so he can get familiar with his surroundings. You should always have an idea of where he is and what he's doing, just in case he's doing something wrong and you can catch him in the act, or if he decides to take off for whatever reason.

When my dogs were pups, I always kept an eye on them when they were loose outside on the property, and was able to recall or interrupt them if I needed to, right away. That way they thought I was always watching them, and it greatly reduced the amount of troubles they could have gotten into. Today I don't always watch them on the property, but I'm sure they still think I am. Additionally, at 10 years old, **they are now the ones watching me all the time**.

As a general rule of thumb, **your GSD is always going to be: a) Supervised and under your control, or b) secured** (in his place, the car, the pen/yard or in the house). Trust me, a Shepherd can disappear real quick when his instincts call, and even though you can't control natural instincts, you can control the dog.

It will be **your responsibility to have control over your dog at all**

times, therefore reducing your exposure to liability and "accidents."

It is my greatest hope that any future owner of a German Shepherd will **seriously consider the training part** of their dog. While some dog breeds (pets) might need little training, the GSD needs to be trained; failure to do so is similar to leaving a loaded gun lying around.

And FINALLY, know that it is going to take time to train, to play and exercise, but it will turn out to **be the best investment of your time**. The first 2-4 months of training will guarantee a beautiful lifelong relationship.

CHAPTER 7: PLAYING AND EXERCISE

Playing with your dog is very important for bonding and communicating, as well as beneficial for his health and digestion.

It is a stress reliever and good for building and keeping muscle mass. Playing is, as I mentioned earlier, an excellent way to establish communication channels, and start the training process.

As you discover your puppy, do your best to pay attention to what are some of your dog's preferred traits. Some might be more into fetching, others into playing hide and seek or roughhousing. If you can identify that, **spend more time playing the games he likes most**. It's hard to communicate and play with a dog who doesn't fetch, so find out what he's into. GSDs almost always like to fetch.

Getting them excited about a ball, for example, will allow you to use that ball as a training tool.

Playing can also be used as a reward very successfully. You can train a dog all day as long as playing is the reward. You'll just get tired before he does.

Talk to your dog a lot. The sound of your voice soothes him, and he will start recognizing words the more he hears them. For example, my dogs recognize a lot more words than I am probably aware of. In some conversations with other people, I have to literally spell out some words like B.E.A.R, so my dogs don't go on full alarm mode if I pronounce that word.

Just like routine, your dog will know when you put your boots on and grab a toy, that it's time to go out and play. Play with your dog a lot, it's actually good for the both of you!

CHAPTER 8: THE WORLD AND OTHERS

GSDs are very curious and engaging by nature. They want to learn about everything they come across and when they are young, they will need supervision and a leash. Do not hesitate to take your GSD into many different environments. **Exposing him to various situations from an early age** will get him familiar with the unfamiliar. Avoid stressful environments and loud noises at first. Keep him close by, and he will be fine knowing you are there.

The GSD is very loyal and will want to be with you all the time. And I mean ALL THE TIME. He doesn't have to be on your lap, but he'll always be happiest being somewhere where he can keep an eye on you. So when traveling, for example, figure out how to have him somewhere where he can see you (or know where you are), when possible.

Think safety: Your job is to assist your GSD in discovering the world and not get hurt in the process. Think about roads, other dogs, wildlife, flying horse hooves, temperatures too hot in the car or too cold outside, etc.

As a puppy, your dog should have lots of interaction with other dogs, and pettings from other humans. This will help him in his early life to be social and not a shy, closet recluse. Your dog should always come across as friendly; don't worry about him guarding you or your property; as he grows, he will sense danger or an ill-intended person all by himself and will react accordingly.

In the real world, someone almost always ends up in your driveway or knocking on your door. **Shepherds are very protective of their environment.** You must have a plan to make sure he doesn't get run over, jump on someone, or bite the mail person.

Hosting guests at home: your GSD should greet them at the door with you so he can get all those fun traveling smells of other pets and where the guests have been. After that, your GSD can go back to his "out-of-the-way" spot. Once there, most Shepherds will prefer being left alone. Keep visitors from going to pet them in their bed. If the guests want to interact, call your dog to come up and visit.

As a general rule, your GSD will have lots of free roaming on your property and in your house. Your dog should be more restricted and under control when off property.

Security perimeter protocol: As I mentioned earlier, I'm not a fan of big dogs in small apartments. I will therefore assume that you will have a good sized (fenced) yard or property. GSDs are as territorial as most dogs, and your dog will need to know the boundaries of the property.

You should walk your desired, observable perimeter with your dog and recall/pull on leash before the last point where you want him to go. With repetition and words of encouragement, he will understand the perimeter. (If it's fenced in, it will be pretty self-explanatory).

For example, when I walk down the driveway to my gate, the dogs do not go beyond the gate, whether it is open or closed. They have learned to stay on the property unless I take them out for a walk.

That said, left unsupervised, my intact male Rio disappeared for a day once because there was a female in heat a mile away. He was 4 years old, and fully trained. Needless to say, my dog was not supervised at that time.

Without supervision, restraint, or locked up in a pen, **nature will override your finely trained dog any day**.

You have been warned.

CHAPTER 9: HEALTH AND CARE

Before you get a puppy, find **a good veterinarian. Ideally, one that has some knowledge of the German Shepherd breed.** I lucked out, my vet not only is familiar with GSDs, she has one, and is also from Germany. She is great.

Find the best puppy food you can afford, and subsequently, the best adult food. Stick to the same brand if you can, as GSDs have fragile digestive systems. Some can be finicky eaters when you change food programs.

Make sure your dog has a bowl of fresh, clean water each day, and that the bowl is cleaned regularly.

Regular walks, play and exercise, as mentioned before, will greatly contribute to good health. Your dog's digestive system will adapt to the regular schedule.

Take the time to inspect your dog's droppings. It says a lot about your dog's general health, and any potential issues can be detected early just by looking at stool. (Plus indicate anything he might have eaten behind your back).

Speaking of stool, **make sure your dog's environment is clean** and that his pen or outdoor areas are regularly picked up. Some dogs, especially puppies, love that recycled "food" taste and great care should be given to keep them from recycling dropping. Just pick up daily or as often as possible.

Give your GSD lots of love, as you would any other pet. Petting your dog often is a stress reliever for the both of you. Bonus: If you bathe them regularly, they not only love water, the towel and the brush, they are much softer to pet (and smell better as well).

Shepherds are the biggest shedders and need regular brushings. (And yes, there is still going to be hair everywhere they go.)

Be aware of extreme heat and cold. A dog can die of heat in a car or freeze his ears off in a very cold environment. I train dogs in the Montana winters, but in below freezing temperatures I limit their exposure. Even though they could take colder temps longer, they're happier next to the wood stove. Me too.

I once had a GSD that traveled everywhere with me, I nicknamed him "planes, trains and sailboats". **Your dog will follow you anywhere**, and I mean anywhere you take him.

Shepherds love to swim. If you're near the ocean, make sure they at least get a fresh water rinse after a salty swim.

Also be aware of the strain caused by jumping in and out of cars or pickup trucks. For as much as your GSD is an athlete and wants to show it off, these repetitive motions will slowly weaken his rear end. I built a ramp out of OSB and carpet for mine that slides in and out of the truck bed.

Basically, to care for a healthy GSD and any dog really, just create a loving relationship. One where **he will trust you and your word 100 percent, and he knows that you also trust him**.

If your dog is well taken care of, given attention, "worked," and well included in the family, he will be happier, and therefore healthier.

That is very important.

CHAPTER 10: MULTIPLE DOGS

You may choose to own 2 GSDs, or already have other dogs of different breeds. Although your GSD may not get along with other members of the pack at first, the dogs will figure out the hierarchy eventually all by themselves. You might have to intervene if it gets out of hand to save yourself a trip to the vet.

I am only going to focus here on more than one GSD, but you might be able to apply some of the following tidbits to other pairs.

Advantages: Having 2 as puppies, they will keep each other company. They also play a lot together, which covers a large part of their exercise program, giving you more time off.

I found the training to be easier, although it takes a little bit more time training one dog at a time.

The beauty is that I can lock one up in the fenced pen so he can watch while I am training the other, then I switch. **That way the dog I am training already knows what we're going to do**, and is eager to show off how smart he is.

That said, I currently have a brother and sister pair from the same litter. This dynamic works for the life of the dogs, whereas if I had had 2 males, there would have been too much competition for my attention, and therefore potential troubles down the line.

Another thing I like about 2 GSDs is that I can keep one to guard the house, and travel with the other one. They can both take turns going or staying, that way I have everything covered. The family is secured at home, and the one family member going somewhere is also covered.

Another advantage is that you get **twice the love, and kisses in stereo**!

Inconveniences: Multiply the food, the Vet bills, and the occasional kennel by 2. Remember, proper dog ownership is not cheap, so if you can barely afford one, don't get 2!

You will need twice as much space: In the house, the car, the yard. You will also have twice the droppings to pick up.

As much as it is easy to train two of them and they can play together, one can often get the other in trouble. Such as taking off through the woods, one is just leading, the other, following.

Never underestimate nature and natural instinct. It will override your dog's brain anytime you let your guard down. **They mean well, they just can't help it!**

Then think long term: It is going to be hard for everyone when one passes away. Your GSD has feelings too, and I do not look forward to that day when one goes, after spending a whole life with the other (and me.)

CHAPTER 11: RETIREMENT

Whether you have a family companion or a working GSD, there comes a time when your dog can officially "retire," so he can enjoy a well-deserved break for his many years of good service and companionship.

I like to start giving my dogs a break around 8-10 years of age, depending on the type of work they have done and how healthy they are. You be the judge, and your vet will no doubt share their good advice if necessary.

What I mean by "retirement" is that from then on I can give my dog more freedom to do what he wants. Cruise through the kitchen if he wants to and overall relax the general rules that he's been living with. He already knows what to do, and what not to do, and doesn't need as much supervision; he knows the basics: Stay off the road, don't eat trash and stick around close by.

My female Frida, for example, finally gets to enjoy the low profile couch; she had been eyeing it for 10 years, and I had to convince her it was ok to get on it. Now she goes there by herself. Reason why, is it is more comfortable than her dog bed, is easier to get on and off, and she has a straight line of sight on the main entry door.

At that time a dog will get more treats, especially in his food bowl, and lots of petting time. It is at an old age that dogs can develop tumors or skin disorders. So pet him often, it will help you detect anything hiding in his furry coat!

Working dogs will miss working on a regular basis, so make sure to include some playtime that is associated with their retired work so they don't miss it too much.

Retirement doesn't mean your GSD just sits around doing nothing. It means that he is done rounding up sheep or sitting in the back of a cruiser; so keep including him on your travels and in your daily routine. He'll still need exercise and play, the amount of which you will determine according to your dog's general health as he ages.

Since you have a few more years with your GSD, start thinking about the day he's going to go to poochie heaven. **Enjoy those years well**, as he will go before you do.

If you are looking to replace your companion or working dog, this would be a good time to consider getting a puppy to overlap with your dog's later years. This is a good way to introduce a new dog, a friend for your current GSD to play with and learn tricks from.

Since your retiring GSD will be well trained and know all the ropes, it will be a matter of just cut and paste for the training of your new dog.

Somehow, dogs know when that time is coming. Bringing a puppy into your life will make your current GSD happy to know that a new guard is coming on duty for you and your family, which he is very attached to.

Sometimes, when Rio stares deeply into my eyes, I get the feeling that he's reading my mind. At other times, I question his psychic abilities to talk to me and tell me what he wants.

I dedicate this little guide book to my teachers:

Sheriff
Fraulein
Bremen
D
Rio
Frida

And to all the Shepherds in the world, past and present. Thank you for all the love and assistance you have brought to people everywhere.

www.ingramcontent.com/pod-product-compliance
Lightning Source LLC
Chambersburg PA
CBHW072339300426
44109CB00042B/1956